New English Parade

Senior Authors

Mario Herrera

Theresa Zanatta

Consulting Authors

Alma Flor Ada   Anna Uhl Chamot   Jim Cummins

Christine Ewy   Carolyn Kessler   J. Michael O'Malley

Writer

Caroline Banks

Longman

Contents

1 Famous People

1. Think and discuss.

1. What is your favourite musical group?
2. Who are your favourite musicians?
3. Have you ever met a famous person?
4. What famous person would you like to meet?

2. Listen. Read.

Act out the conversation.

Lin: I can't believe it. I just can't believe it!

Tony: Believe what? What's the matter with your hand?

Lin: Nothing's the matter. This hand is famous.

Tony: What?

Lin: Chick shook my hand after the performance last night. I'm—I'm so—I'm so excited! I can't even talk!

Tony: Well, let me shake your hand.

Lin: OK. Then your hand will be famous too!

Tony: Who wants to shake *my* hand now?

3. Listen and sing.

This is Chick and the Chicklettes' most famous song.

Walking down the street,
Thinking of you,
Looking up at the stars and the moon.

Oops! Oooo!
I'm so mad.
I've got chewing gum on my shoe!

Chew, chew, chew!
Shoe, shoe, shoe!
Chewing gum on my shoe!

4. Read and match.

A reporter interviewed Chick for a magazine. This is part of the interview. Match the interview questions with Chick's answers. Write the missing question.

I met a famous person once!

A. What was your first hit song?

B. Did you go to music college?

C. _____

_____

_____I got a set of drums for my tenth birthday. After that, I spent a lot of my free time playing the drums.

_____ Yes. After I finished school, I went to a special college to study music. I always knew that I wanted to be a musician.

_____ We had our first hit song about five years ago. It was "Chewing Gum on My Shoe." Actually, it was the first song that our group wrote and played together.

5. Read the biography.

Do you know Wallace and Gromit? Who are they?

Nick Park was born in 1958. As a child, he loved to watch cartoons and to draw. Nick's school books were full of cartoons. One teacher said, "Park, you will never make a living out of cartoons."

Nick always wanted to entertain people. When he was 13, Nick began his first film. Nick used his mother's film camera and he made the film in one week.

At the age of 15, Nick became famous in his school. He entered the BBC Young Animators film competition. He did not win, but the film appeared on television. After leaving school, Nick went to college to study art. In the summer holidays, he got a job in a factory. In 1974, he bought a new and better film camera with the money from his job.

In 1982, Nick invented his most famous characters, Wallace and Gromit. He created them out of plasticine, a special kind of clay. Wallace is an inventor. He lives with his dog Gromit, at 62 West Wallaby Street. Wallace is always cheerful—if there is some cheese in the fridge!

The first Wallace and Gromit film, *A Grand Day Out*, appeared in 1989. It won many awards around the world. Then came *The Wrong Trousers* in 1992. The characters of Shaun the sheep, Wendolene Ramsbottom and her dog, Preston, joined Wallace and Gromit in the third film, *A Close Shave*, in 1995. Wallace and Gromit aren't Nick Park's only characters. In 2000, he and Peter Lord made *Chicken Run* and introduced many new characters including two chickens called Rocky and Bunty.

Today, children and adults all over the world can enjoy Nick Park's stories in cinemas and on videos.

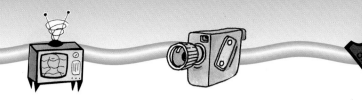

6. Read and number.

Put the events in the correct order.

_____ Nick created Wallace and Gromit from plasticine.

_____ Nick worked in a factory.

_____ Nick became famous in his school.

_____ Nick Park was born.

_____ Wallace and Gromit appeared in three films.

_____ Nick got a new film camera.

_____ Nick made his first film.

Can you add to the lists?

7. Read and write.

Complete the time line.

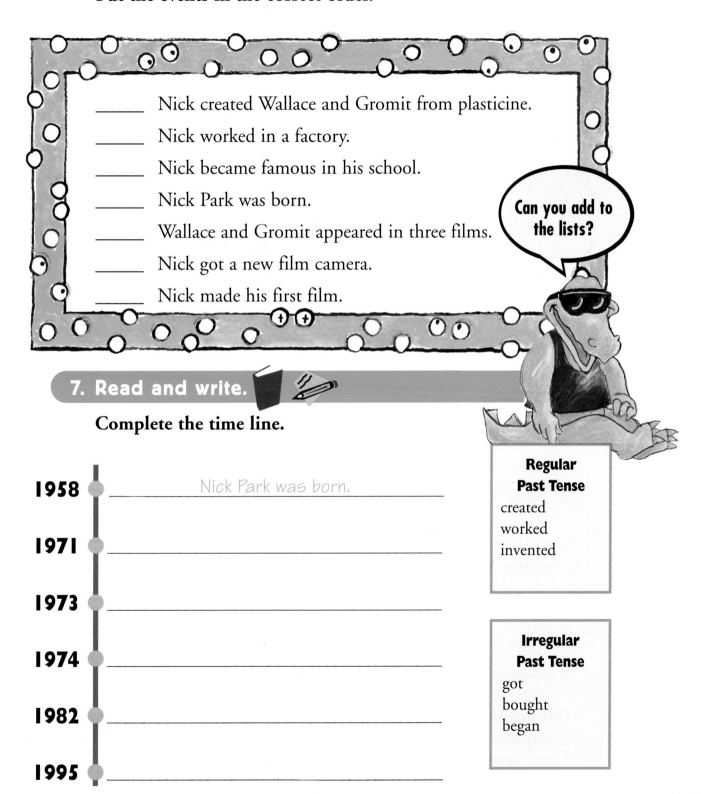

1958	Nick Park was born.
1971	_____
1973	_____
1974	_____
1982	_____
1995	_____

Regular Past Tense
created
worked
invented

Irregular Past Tense
got
bought
began

8. Listen.

Put the dates on the time line.

She was the first woman to fly alone from England to Australia.
_____

She was the first pilot to fly from England to Moscow in one day.
_____

She began her last flight.
_____

Amy Johnson was born.
_____

She got her pilot's licence.
_____

9. Make your own time line.

Fill in the events and the years.

1. When were you born? _____

2. When did you start school? _____

3. When did you start to study English? _____

4. What is the present year? _____

What an interesting life!

List three important things that happened in your life. Write the year that each happened.

1. _____ _____

2. _____ _____

3. _____ _____

Cut out the time line on page 93.
Complete it with the information above.
Share your time line with the class.

Gloria Estefan

by Judy Nayer

You can hear Gloria Estefan on the radio. You can see her on your TV. Today, she is one of the world's favourite singers. But her life was not always so wonderful.

Gloria had a very difficult childhood. She was born in Cuba in 1958. In 1959, Gloria and her mother moved to Miami in the U.S.A. It was difficult for them to live alone and they had little money. All their money went to buy food.

Gloria, with the band, N'Sync

Emilio, Gloria and son, Nayib

One day, something terrible happened. Gloria, Emilio and their son were travelling in the band's bus. A van hit them. Gloria's back was broken in the accident. Her family was afraid she would not walk. It took a long time for Gloria to get better. But after ten months, Gloria was singing.

Gloria continues to write music and sing. She has created many hit songs and albums in her career. She and Emilio bought a beautiful house in Miami. Gloria and Emilio live there with their son, Nayib, and their daughter, Emily Marie.

Gloria wanted to grow up and make life better for herself and others. And that is what she did.

Gloria decided that when she grew up, she would make her life better. Gloria did not know any English before she went to school. But she worked hard at school. Soon she knew English very well.

After two years, Gloria's father left Cuba, too, and joined them in Florida. But soon he left to fight in the Vietnam War. When he returned from the war, he was ill. Gloria had to help take care of him.

Gloria believed in herself. She loved music and began to write songs, sing and play the guitar.

One day a musical group, the Miami Latin Boys, came to her school. Gloria met a musician in the band—Emilio Estefan. He was from Cuba, too. He helped Gloria and her friends start a band to entertain at a party.

Then Gloria went to university. One day, Gloria went to a wedding. The Miami Latin Boys were playing there. Emilio asked Gloria to sing with the band. The audience enjoyed her performance. Emilio asked Gloria to be in the band. Gloria was excited, but she wanted to finish university. So she just sang at weekends. After she graduated, Gloria sang with the band all the time.

The band changed its name to Miami Sound Machine. And Gloria and Emilio had their own wedding. Gloria wrote many popular songs. The band became famous and won many music awards.

PROJECT

Interview a famous person.

Brainstorm a list of famous people with your class. Then work with a classmate. Choose a famous person, living or dead, to interview.

1. Read about the famous person.
2. Make a time line of important dates and events in the person's life.
3. Write interview questions.
4. Practise the interview. Take turns being the famous person and the interviewer.
5. Give your interview in front of the class.

Where and when were you born?

Where did you grow up?

How did you become famous?

Do you like being famous? Why or why not?

Make a puppet character.

Use an old sock, cloth or paper. Make a face for your puppet. Think about what your puppet is like. Answer these questions:

1. What is your puppet's name?
2. When was your puppet "born"?
3. How would you describe your puppet? Is your puppet friendly? Is it clever?
4. What are four exciting or interesting things that happened in your puppet's life?

Choose a partner and make your puppets interview each other about their lives.

Who's your favourite puppet?

Are you still living?

Did you speak English?

Did you play sports?

Were you the leader of a country?

Play Twenty Questions.

1. Work in small groups. Each of you takes a turn choosing to be a famous person.
2. The group asks questions to guess the famous person. The questions should be ones answered by yes or no.
3. See how many questions the group asks before they guess the famous person. They can ask up to twenty questions.

Mona Lisa
Painting by da Vinci about 1500

Gromit
A plasticine dog 1982—

Sir Paul McCartney
Singer 1942—

William Shakespeare
Writer 1564–1616

Emma Thompson
Film actress 1959—

Pelé
Football player 1940—

Elizabeth II
Queen of Britain 1926—

Mother Teresa
Humanitarian 1910–1997

Marie Curie
Scientist 1867–1934

Akihito
Emperor of Japan 1933—

Gary Sobers
Cricketer 1936—

✓ Read the story.

Complete the time line.

What do sharks, dinosaurs and creatures from outer space have in common? Steven Spielberg, the film director, of course. He made hit films on all these subjects.

Born in 1947, Spielberg became interested in films at an early age. He began his directing career in 1969, directing scary films for TV. Killer sharks were the subject of his first big film hit, *Jaws,* in 1975. The film was exciting and filled with action. The sharks seemed real!

In 1982, Spielberg had an even bigger success with the story of E.T., a friendly visitor to Earth from outer space. This film made more money than any other until 1993. In that year, a film topped it. What was it? It was another film by Spielberg named *Jurassic Park.* In this film, dinosaurs once again walked the earth. In 1997, he made another hit film, *The Lost World*, a follow-up to *Jurassic Park.* Of the ten most popular films in film history, Spielberg has made four. This is quite a record!

Why doesn't he make a film about alligators?

1975

| Spielberg was born. | _____ _____ _____ | He made *E.T.* | _____ _____ _____ | _____ _____ _____ |

✓ My Journal

1. The most interesting person I learnt about in this unit was

_____ because _____

_____.

2. A person I would like to learn more about is _____

because _____.

2 My Story

1. Think and discuss.

1. Have you ever done anything exciting? What was it?
2. Has anything scary ever happened to you? What was it?

2. Fill in the questionnaire.

Get ready to share information.

I've never ridden a horse.

Finish the sentences.

1. My favourite free-time activity is _____
2. My favourite subject at school is _____ .
_____ .

Circle the answer.

1. Have you ever been on TV?
2. Have you ever gone to a concert?
3. Have you ever ridden a horse?
4. Have you ever had a pet?
5. Have you ever seen a scary film?

Yes, I have.	No, I haven't.
Yes, I have.	No, I haven't.
Yes, I have.	No, I haven't.
Yes, I have.	No, I haven't.
Yes, I have.	No, I haven't.

3. Share information.

Work with a partner. Ask about one another.
What information has your partner given in the questionnaire?

4. Read Wayne's pen friend letter.

What does he say about himself?

Dear Ana,

My name is Wayne Yun, and I am twelve years old. I live in Wales. I was born in Korea and came to Bangor when I was three. I speak Korean and English. I've studied Spanish for a year, but I can't speak it very well.

My favourite sport is cricket. I've played for my school team for three years. I like to bowl and bat. Do you play for a sports team?

I like to go sailing with my grandfather. We started racing a year ago and we've won six races. I fell off the boat once. It was really scary! My grandfather threw me a rope and helped me back into the boat. Luckily I always wear a life jacket!

I hope you'll write to me soon.

Your friend,

Wayne

5. Think. Remember. Say.

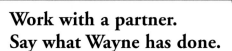

**Work with a partner.
Say what Wayne has done.**

live in Wales
He's lived in Wales for nine years.

study Spanish
play for a cricket team
race sailing boats
number of races won

Language Note

I've = I have
We've = We have
He's = He has
She's = She has
They've = They have

6. Listen to Ana.

Circle the topics Ana is going to write about in her letter to Wayne.

Her pet   A scary thing that has happened

Languages she knows   An exciting thing that has happened

A trip to the beach   Favourite school subjects

7. Read and complete.

Write the correct form of the verb on the line.

> **Language Note**
> Present perfect
> have + past participle
> have + done
> have + learnt

Dear Wayne,

    Thanks for your letter. I'm eleven. I ___have lived___ in Peru all my life. I _____ English in school since I was five. I also speak Spanish and a little French. I have a younger brother.

    I don't play for a sports team. I play in a band. I _____ saxophone in my school band for two years. The most exciting thing I _____ ever _____ is to play the saxophone on TV!

    Do you have any pets? My family _____ _____ Chispa, our parrot, for thirteen years. Chispa is very smart. He speaks Spanish well, and he _____ to speak a little English! He can say "hello," "goodbye" and "have a nice day."

    Write to me soon.

            Your pen friend,

            Ana

> **Word Bank**
> do   live
> have   play
> learn   study

8. Write the answers.

Talk with a partner. Share more information about yourself.

1. How long have you studied English?

_____

2. How long have you known your best friend?

_____

3. How long have you had the same hairstyle?

_____

9. Write your own pen friend letter.

Write a letter to Wayne or Ana. Talk with a partner about what you are going to write about yourself.

10. Listen. Sing.

Have you ever eaten snails, Melvin Roy, Melvin Roy?
Have you ever eaten snails, Melvin Roy?
No, I haven't had a snail,
I would rather try a whale.
It's a sad thing I cannot eat a snail.

Have you ever been to Rome, Nancy Joy, Nancy Joy?
Have you ever been to Rome, Nancy Joy?
No, I haven't been to Rome.
I would rather stay at home.
It's a sad thing I will not leave my home.

Can you add another verse?

11. Complete the survey.

With your class, add two questions to the survey.

> Have you ever climbed a mountain?

Can you find someone in your class who has . . . ?

Name

climbed a mountain? _____

visited a film set? _____

been to an amusement park? _____

gone to a football match? _____

played the piano? _____

talked to a famous person? _____

bought a present for a friend? _____

taken care of a small child? _____

won a prize or an award? _____

forgotten to do homework? _____

lost a key? _____

made a model aeroplane? _____

_____ _____

_____ _____

> How many of these have you done?

The Storm

by Cheyenne Cisco

I don't get angry often. But I *did* get angry last summer. You see, that was when the big storm blew into town. It was the biggest storm I have ever seen. It was the biggest storm ever! I can never forget it. The storm blew the doors off. But I've lost doors before. It blew all the windows out. But I like it windy. It blew all the grass away. But then I didn't have to mow the lawn!

Then that storm blew my lamp up in the air. My watermelon lamp! I would not let any storm take my watermelon lamp. I got angry!

I got home late that night. And I saw what a mess the storm made. My saxophone was in the climbing frame. My parrot was in the chest of drawers. My bath was in a tree. And I've never forgotten that kangaroo in my swimming pool!

But I decided to take care of all that in the morning. I wasn't angry. I had my lamp. And do you know what? It still worked!

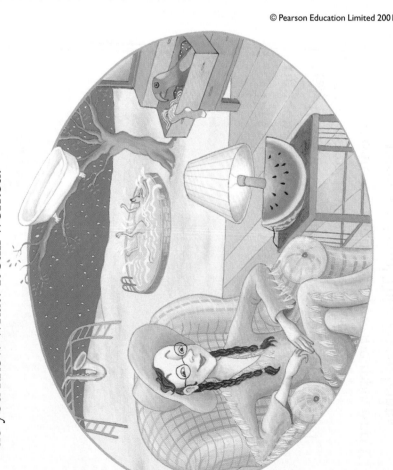

I watched my lamp fly over the ocean. That storm moved fast. I just had time to throw on a life jacket and get my saddle and some rope.

At the beach, I whistled to a big old whale. I put my saddle on it and jumped on. I've ridden a whale before—but never in a storm. It was fun.

What a race we had! We went past two sailing boats and a submarine. "We've got to catch that storm! We've got to get that watermelon lamp!" I shouted.

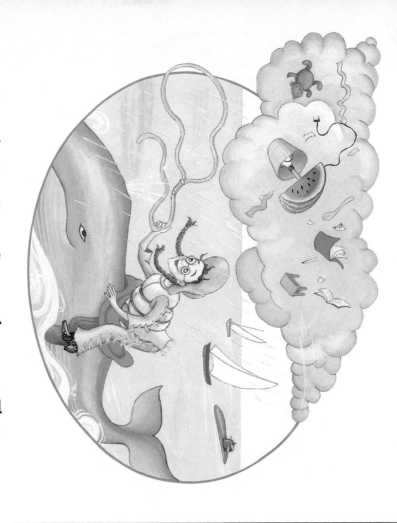

That whale was a winner. What a race! It swam right under the storm cloud. I studied the dark cloud. Yes, it was time to throw my rope. And I got the storm! It was an exciting time!

I held onto my saddle. I threw the rope. And I got my watermelon lamp! Then I went home.

PROJECT

Make a personal memory box.

1. Collect things that show who you are.
2. Decorate a shoe box. Name it "My Memory Box." Put things you collected inside. Show your box to the class or a small group. Talk about the things in it.

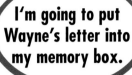

I'm going to put Wayne's letter into my memory box.

Work with a partner. Brainstorm for ideas to write about. Complete the exercise below.

List two exciting things that have happened to you.

1. _____

2. _____

List two scary things that have happened to you.

1. _____

2. _____

Choose one of these to write about.
Put your story into your memory box.

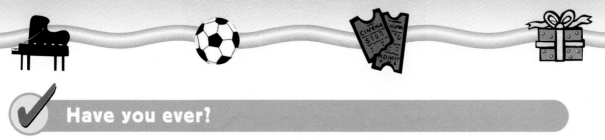

✓ Have you ever?

1. Work with a partner. Cut out the counters and cards on page 95. Mix up both sets of cards and place them face-down.
2. Take turns picking a card and asking your partner the question: *Have you ever been on a train?*
3. When you answer yes, move your counter the number of spaces on the card. The first player to get to "Finish" wins.

Think and write.

Use the ideas in the box. Add two of your own.

IDEA BOX: climb a tree   be in a swimming pool
ride a bike   jump from a plane

Things I Have Done

1. I have _____ .

2. I have _____ .

3. I have _____ .

Things I Haven't Done

1. I haven't _____ .

2. I haven't _____ .

3. I haven't _____ .

My Journal

1. My earliest memory is when I _____

_____ .

2. Words that describe me are _____, _____

and _____ .

3. One thing I haven't done that I want to do is to _____

_____ .

4. Now that I have completed this unit, I can _____

_____ .

3 Jobs

1. Think and discuss.

1. What do you want to be when you grow up?
2. What jobs have people in your family got?

2. Find out about a partner.

What does your partner like doing? Tick Yes or No.

Partner's Name:	Yes	No
teaching people how to do things		
drawing pictures		
working with tools or machinery		
doing the same thing again and again		
creating new ideas		
solving problems		
writing		
working with numbers		

3. Think about yourself.

Circle three things that describe you. Then work with a partner. Say why you circled the words. Discuss which jobs you might be good at doing.

creative   mathematical   mechanical   persuasive
helpful   hardworking   careful   energetic

I can't decide what I want to be.

PEANUTS reprinted by permission of UFS, Inc.

4. Listen. Read.

Act out the conversation.

How many different jobs do the students talk about?

Andy: When I was little, I wanted to be a firefighter. What did you want to be?

Kate: A ballet dancer. Now I'm not sure what I want to be. Dad has told me he'd like me to be a doctor like he is. And Mum is a lawyer, so she wants me to be one too.

Andy: Yes, my parents want me to work in their construction business. But do you know what?

Kate: What?

Andy: I want to be a cook and have my own restaurant. I'm very good at cooking.

Kate: What a coincidence! I'm interested in cooking too. Let's start a restaurant together.

Andy: Great! I'll do the cooking, if you wash the dishes.

Kate: Are you joking? No way!

> **Language Note**
> good at + _____ing
> good at cooking
>
> interested in + _____ing
> interested in cooking

5. Discuss.

1. What did Kate and Andy want to be when they were little?
2. What did you want to be when you were little?
   Have you changed your mind? Why or why not?

6. Read about careers.

Do any of the jobs interest you? Discuss with a partner.

If you are good at speaking English, you may want to become a TRANSLATOR.

TRANSLATORS work for governments and businesses. Some translators work with written materials. Others translate as a person is speaking. These translators must talk and listen at the same time. They really have to think on their feet.

If you are good at writing, you might become a NEWSPAPER REPORTER.

Newspaper reporters usually get information from other people. Their facts must be correct. They use the information to write interesting articles. Reporters need to write quickly. The newspaper has to come out the next day!

Reporters write about sports, news and entertainment. Which kind of reporting interests you?

If you like working with animals, you might become a vet.

Vets are animal doctors. They take care of animals when they are ill. Animals can't say what's wrong with them. But with experience, vets learn to recognise animals' problems. To become a vet, you must study at a special veterinary college.

7. Describe more jobs.

Write a job that matches each skill. Some skills are useful for more than one job. Make sure you use *a* or *an* before each job name.

actor	mechanic	teacher	computer programmer
advertisement writer	nurse	vet	fashion designer
shop assistant	secretary	engineer	carpenter

1. If you like working with people, you might become _____.

2. If you are good at writing, you might become _____.

3. If you are good at working with tools, you might become

   _____.

4. If you are good at drawing, you might become _____.

5. If you are good at working carefully without making

   mistakes, you might become _____.

6. If you are good at selling things or ideas, you might

   become _____.

7. If you like creating new things or ideas, you

   might become _____.

> I'm good at sunning myself.

8. Share your work.

**Work with a group.
Compare answers to Activity 7.**

9. Find a job for you.

Answer the questions. Put a tick if your answer is yes.

1

Are you good at . . .
_____ working with numbers?
_____ working carefully without making mistakes?
_____ understanding written directions?
_____ solving problems?

Are you interested in . . .
_____ working with computers?
_____ working at a desk most of the day?
_____ working both in a group and by yourself?

If you ticked at least four things, consider these jobs:
accountant, computer specialist, researcher, engineer, scientist, architect

Circle the one you might like to do.

> I'm good at doing everything. So what do I do?

2

Are you good at . . .
_____ creating things?
_____ drawing?
_____ working with your hands?
_____ working with tools?

Are you interested in . . .
_____ working by yourself?
_____ selling your ideas to others?

If you ticked at least four things, consider these jobs:
artist, jewellery designer, fashion designer, interior decorator, photographer

Circle the one you might like to do.

3

Are you good at . . .
_____ understanding other people's problems and ideas?
_____ solving problems?
_____ thinking on your feet?

Are you interested in . . .
_____ helping other people?
_____ working with others all day?
_____ studying and reading a lot?

If you ticked at least three things, consider these jobs:
sports teacher, nurse, doctor, police officer

Circle the one you might like to do.

4

Are you good at . . .
_____ playing sports?
_____ working with your hands or body?

Are you interested in . . .
_____ doing exciting things?
_____ working outdoors?
_____ doing physical exercise?

If you ticked at least three things, consider these jobs:

athlete, construction worker, firefighter, racing car driver, forest ranger, sports teacher, dancer

Circle the one you might like to do.

CLOWNING AROUND

by Tess Silver

I am an actor, but I do not appear on a stage. I am an athlete, but I don't play football. I am a dancer, but I am not in the ballet. I've got a camera, but I am not a photographer. I am an artist, but I don't paint.

I am a clown!

In time, working became fun. We all learned special acts. One clown was a bus driver. Inside a tiny bus were twelve clowns!

Another clown carried a briefcase. When he opened it, a bird flew out!

For my favourite trick I used a camera. When I pushed the button—surprise!—water came out.

Come and watch me. Smile, laugh and cheer with us. We have so much fun and never think about how hard we are working. Next time you see a clown, remember that it's not easy, but it's all worth it when you make people happy.

I became interested in clowns when I was little. I went to a party where a clown entertained us. He was so energetic! He had so many creative ideas! "If I become a clown," I thought, "I might make people happy." After his act I asked him, "How can I become a clown?"

"To be a clown," he said, "you have to be hardworking and energetic. There is a lot to learn."

"Hardworking?" I asked. "I thought it would be fun to be a clown."

"It is fun," he said. "It's fun to make people laugh. But it takes practice to be good at it. Today clowns often go to college to learn their tricks."

I knew doctors and scientists had to study a lot. I didn't know clowns did, too. But I wanted that to be my career, so when I grew up I went to clown college.

It was an exciting experience. All the teachers were clowns.

First they showed us how to paint our faces. My clown face is white with a big red mouth. Then we practised tricks. The clowns showed us how to walk on stilts and how to ride a unicycle. If you weren't careful, you fell off. I fell many times before I became any good at it!

PROJECT

Listen and tick.

Yesterday was "Take Our Daughters to Work Day." Carla and Roseanne are talking about going to their parents' jobs. Tick which skills each parent needs for his or her job.

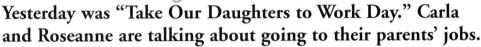

1. Roseanne's mother
   _____ talking with people
   _____ explaining new ideas
   _____ drawing
   _____ working with tools
   _____ selling

2. Carla's father
   _____ working with animals
   _____ talking to groups
   _____ writing
   _____ working carefully
   _____ understanding science

Find out about a job.

Interview an adult about his or her job. Find out what the person does. Ask about the skills the person needs to be good at to do the job. Complete the chart.

PERSON'S NAME	JOB
JOB ACTIVITIES	
SKILLS	

Make a career poster.

On your poster:
1. Write your name.
2. Write three things you are good at doing.
3. Write two school subjects you are good at.
4. Write three jobs you are interested in.
Add drawings or photos to complete your poster.

Career ladders

1. Follow the instructions on page 97.
2. Work with a partner. Take turns picking number cards.
3. If you land on a red space, try to match the job with one of your skill cards and make a sentence: *If you are good at typing, become a secretary.* If you make a match, take two stars. Put the skill card face-down.
4. The winner has the most stars after both players pass "Finish."

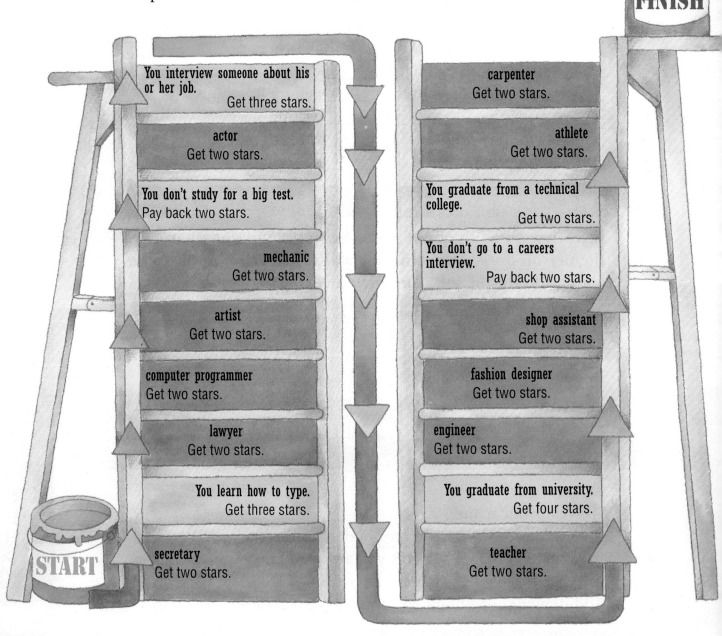

✔ Write some career advice.

Give some career advice to the person with each of these skills.

good at working with animals
If you're good at working with animals, become a vet.

1. good at working with machinery

   _____

2. good at solving problems

   _____

3. good at organising information

   _____

4. good at explaining new ideas

   _____

✔ Write about your career.

I've been working on the railways.

Write the name of a job you like. Then list two skills you've got for that job.

Job: _____

Skills: _____

_____

✔ My Journal

1. A job I'd like to know more about is _____ because

   _____.

2. Now that I have completed this unit, I can _____

   _____.

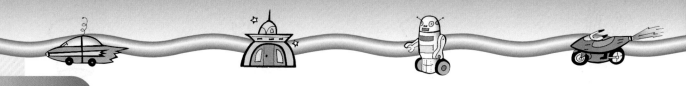

4 The Future

1. Think and discuss

1. How will the world be different twenty years from now?
2. What are two things that may be invented in the next twenty years?
3. What is one thing that may be the same in twenty years as it is now?

2. Imagine your future.

Where will you be in twenty years? Make predictions about yourself. Compare them with a classmate's predictions.

> I think life in the future will be exciting.

My Life —Twenty Years from Now

Twenty years from now the year will be _____

I will be _____ years old.

My job will be _____

I will travel to work in a _____

I'll live in _____

I'll live with _____

My favourite hobby will be _____

I'll get the news of the world from _____

3. Discover life in the future.

Read the magazine article. Find three things that might make life different in the future. Discuss them with a partner.

Welcome to the Future!
Life in the Year 2022

Transport

How will people travel in the future? Many experts think that a traveller will get into a car and tell the car computer where to go. The computer will then drive the car down the road at a speed of 120 miles (202 kilometres) per hour. The computer will be able to sense other cars on the road so that cars won't hit one another.

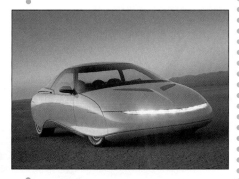

Schools

Schools of the future may be open twelve months a year, twenty-four hours a day, with students coming and going whenever they want. Classrooms will have a computer at every desk.

In fact, some experts think that books might disappear. Students will be able to get information by asking a computer. The computer will give information in video, sounds and words.

TVs in the Home

The TV of the future will show pictures in three dimensions. People will be able to see all the sides of

an object. Some TVs may even sense what the viewer might want to watch and turn themselves on automatically. And people will be able to watch programmes from all over the world at any time of the day or night.

Do you know what these words mean?
speed
to disappear

4. Imagine the future.

Write sentences. Use *will, won't, may, might* or *could*.

electric cars

In twenty years, people will travel in electric cars.

1. school all year long

_____

2. jeans

_____

3. rock music

_____

4. robots in the home

_____

5. flying cars

_____

5. Listen to the radio programme.

Everyone is talking about the future. Tick the things that the professor on the radio programme says will happen in the future.

____ 1. There will be many new inventions to make life easier.
____ 2. There will be no more cars.
____ 3. There will be robots in homes.
____ 4. There will be plant farms in the sea.
____ 5. Rubbish will disappear.
____ 6. People will live in houses on the sea.

6. Write and talk about the future.

What does each picture say about the future? Write your ideas.
Draw two pictures of your own. Share your ideas with a partner.

1. _____

2. _____

3. _____

4. _____

5. _____

6. _____

7. Listen. Read the poem.

2082: Twenty Eighty-Two

What will we do in twenty eighty-two?
What will the world be like?
Will we drive to Mars in flying cars
Or ride rocket-powered bikes to the stars?

What will we do in twenty eighty-two?
What will the world be like?
Will we read magazines on video screens
And still wear baggy, cut-off jeans?

8. Do a future survey.

What do you and your classmates think life will be like in eighty years? Do a survey. Mark each item. Add items of your own on a separate piece of paper. Then count how many classmates answer *Yes* and how many answer *No*. Find the percentages.

Number of students in survey _____	Yes	No	Percentage of Yeses	Nos
In eighty years				
1. People will go on holiday to the moon.	____	____	____	____
2. Most people will speak three languages.	____	____	____	____
3. People will have mechanical pets.	____	____	____	____
4. There will be no books to read.	____	____	____	____
5. People will live in space on space stations.	____	____	____	____

Write a report on the results of the survey.

Report on My Class's Future Survey
In my class, 55% of the students think that in eighty years people will still wear jeans. And 45% think that people won't still wear jeans.

JULES VERNE
Looks into the Future
by Susan McCloskey

Many people try to predict the future. Most cannot do it very well. One person who did make many predictions that came true was the French writer Jules Verne. Verne lived from 1828 to 1905. The plane wasn't invented yet. Wind still powered ships. But in Verne's books people travelled to the moon in a rocket-powered spaceship and sailed under the ocean in a submarine.

What inventions do you think might appear in the future? A machine that will make you disappear? Cars that will speed down highways with no one in them? Plant farms that will feed the world? Automatic robots that will mine for metal? Space stations where people can live for years? Write down your ideas. Add them to a time capsule. You can bury the time capsule with your predictions in it. Then one day many, many years from now, someone can open up the time capsule and check your predictions. Which predictions will come true? Only time will tell.

In Verne's day, many houses had only candlelight. But Verne saw a time when light could be made by electricity. He described planes and predicted computers, television, films and many other mechanical inventions.

But some of Verne's predictions have not come true. Trains still cannot travel at speeds of 1,600 kilometres per hour as he had predicted.

How did Verne get to be such an expert on the future? He said that he learned as much information about the present as he could. He talked about some of his ideas with professors. He read about science and put these ideas into his books. As a result, ideas that seemed new and strange to some of his readers were known to scientists and inventors of his day.

PROJECT

Think future! Make a time capsule.

A time capsule shows what life is like at a certain time. People put things into the time capsule. In the future, other people open the time capsule and learn about life at that time.

What are some interesting things you could put in a time capsule?

Work in groups. Brainstorm for a list. Here is a start.

Roller blades
Baggy jeans

Pocket computer
Photos of your class or school

_____

_____

_____

_____

_____

_____

For your group's time capsule, decide on each of these:
1. A box or container to use
2. What pictures or things to put in the capsule
3. Where to put the time capsule

Cut out the label on page 99. Complete it and stick it on your capsule.

Imagine and make predictions.

Work in small groups. What will your classmates be doing in twenty years?

I'll be the best skater in the world.

1. Who will be the leader of your country?
2. Who will speak five languages?
3. Who will be famous?
4. Who will live in a different country?
5. Who will be rich?

Radio interview: Life in the future

**Be radio producers! Plan a radio interview programme.
Work in small groups.**

1. Decide on these roles:
   - ▨ The radio programme host
   - ▨ The radio programme guest who will be an expert on life in the future and will make predictions
   - ▨ Two or three callers to the radio show

2. Next, choose a topic about life in the future. Here are some ideas:
   - ✖ Transport　　　✖ Schools　　✖ Houses　　✖ Food

3. Write questions on the topic. The callers will ask the questions. Here are some ideas:

   ✔ How will people travel?　　　✔ What will schools be like?

   ✔ How will houses be different?　✔ What will people eat?

These vegetable pills are great!

4. Then brainstorm predictions about the topic. Write down at least five predictions. The radio programme guest may use them as answers.

5. Rehearse the interview. What questions will the callers ask? How will the guest expert answer the questions?

6. Present your programme in front of the class.

Complete the article.

How well can you make predictions?

Homes of the future (1. have) _____ many new inventions to make life easier. People (2. use) _____ one computer to give instructions to a large number of machines in the house. The machines (3. do) _____ all the chores. Robot-like machines (4. clean) _____ the house. Food (5. be) _____ in plastic packages. People or robots (6. warm) _____ up the packages.

Juice, please.

Make predictions.

1. In twenty years, schools _____
_____.

2. In twenty years, I _____
_____.

My Journal

1. The most interesting invention I read about in this unit was _____
_____.

2. I am now able to talk about _____
_____.

5 The Planets

1. Think and discuss.

1. Would you like to travel in space one day? Say why.
2. How many planets are there?
3. What are the names of the planets in your language?

Sun   Mercury Venus Earth Mars   Jupiter   Saturn   Uranus   Neptune   Pluto

2. Learn about the solar system.

Look at the diagram. Fill in the chart.

Which two planets are closest to Earth?
Which planet is further from Earth—Uranus or Pluto?

Planet	Distance from the Sun	One Orbit of the Sun
Mercury	36 million miles (58 million kilometres)	88 days
_____	67 million miles (108 million kilometres)	225 days
Earth	93 million miles (150 million kilometres)	365 days
_____	141 million miles (228 million kilometres)	687 days
Jupiter	484 million miles (778 million kilometres)	12 years
_____	888 million miles (1,429 million kilometres)	29 years
_____	1,786 million miles (2,875 million kilometres)	84 years
Neptune	2,799 million miles (4,504 million kilometres)	165 years
_____	3,666 million miles (5,900 million kilometres)	248 years

3. Learn more about the planets.

Which fact is the most interesting? Discuss with a partner.

Venus's temperature is blisteringly hot at 462°C. Thick poisonous clouds block out the sun. It's dark and gloomy.

The red colour of **Mars** comes from the iron-rich dust of its surface. If you weighed 45 kilograms on Earth, you would weigh only 17 kilograms on Mars.

Mercury is a rocky sphere. It rotates slowly, so its days are very long. If you lived on Mercury, one day would be equal to 59 days on Earth.

If I lived on Mars, I'd be so-o-o light!

Jupiter, the largest planet, is a hot ball of gas and liquid. It's so large that 1,300 Earths could fit inside. It is now known that Jupiter has thin rings around it and sixteen moons. The largest moon is bigger than Mercury.

Pluto is the coldest, smallest and furthest planet in our solar system. Astronomers guessed that Pluto existed before they actually saw it through a telescope.

It's very windy on **Saturn**. The temperature is -178°C. Saturn's seven rings are made of billions of pieces of ice.

Scientists have recently found rings on **Uranus** and **Neptune**. These planets look blue because of the gases in their atmosphere. Planet **Earth** is blue too.

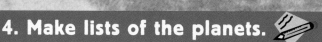

4. Make lists of the planets.

Work with a partner. Use the information on page 42.

1. List the planets in order of their size. Begin with the smallest planet and end with the largest.
2. List the planets in order of the time it takes to orbit the sun. Begin with the longest orbit and end with the shortest.

5. Create and answer questions.

Work with a partner.
Use the diagram and chart
on page 42. Write ten
questions. Then work with
another set of partners.
Share your questions. Take
turns asking and answering
your questions. Here are
some examples:

Comparative:
This is *smaller* than that.
Which is *larger*— this or that?
Which is *further* from the sun—this or that?

Superlative:
It is the *smallest* of all.
Which one is *furthest* from the sun?

Which planets are smaller than Venus?
Which planet is the furthest from the sun?

6. Remember the planet names.

How can you remember the planets in order from the sun? Learn this silly sentence. Can you explain how the sentence will help you?

My Very Excited Monkey Just Slid Under Nathan's Piano.

7. Listen to the astronomer.

If you weighed 45 kilograms, how much would you weigh on each planet?

I weigh 90kg on Earth.

Fantastic!

Planet	Weight
Venus	____ kilograms
Mars	____ kilograms
Jupiter	____ kilograms
Saturn	____ kilograms

8. How long would a year be?

Use the chart on page 42. Say how long your year would be on each planet.

Language Note

If + past, would + verb
If I lived on Mars, my year would be 687 days long.

1. Pluto _____

_____

2. Venus _____

_____

3. Jupiter _____

_____

4. Mercury _____

_____

9. Listen. Sing.

I'd Like to Ride a Comet
I'd like to ride a comet.
It would be a lot of fun
To shoot off into space and meet
The children of the sun.

10. Imagine a trip to a planet.

Talk with a partner about travelling in space: Where would you go?
How would you get there? What would you see? What problems
might you have?

Now read the story of an imaginary trip.

As our spaceship got nearer to Jupiter, the orange and yellow surface of the planet filled the ship's windows. It was an awesome sight! Now we were passing Jupiter's rings and some of Jupiter's moons. The moon Io looked like a giant pizza, covered with red, white and brown spots. On it, volcanoes were throwing out plumes of red. In contrast, the moon Europa had a dead, icy surface. Suddenly, ahead we could see Jupiter's Great Red Spot. This large windstorm was moving swiftly. We were getting closer and closer to the planet's surface of gas. How near would our spaceship get to the planet's stormy surface?

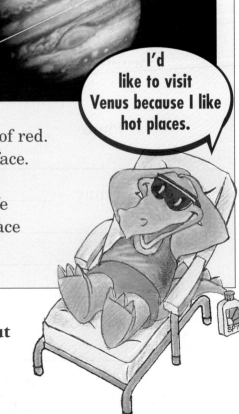

I'd like to visit Venus because I like hot places.

Find more information about the planet
you would like to visit. Talk or write about
your trip to the planet.

The New Planet

by Marie Fonda

Alonzo turned on the food machine in the spaceship. He pushed the button for PIZZA. "Would you like some lunch?" he asked.

"I would rather finish this first," said Julia. "Can you help me check the distances to Jupiter, Saturn, Uranus and Neptune before you eat?"

Alonzo and Julia were going to Pluto for summer camp. There was a machine on Pluto that changed its atmosphere. It made Pluto's weather very much like Earth's—only better! It was the best camp in the solar system. And it was the furthest they had ever been from Earth.

Julia turned from the computer. She looked at Alonzo. She smiled. "If you weren't so hungry, you would not be seeing that planet," she said.

"What?" Alonzo asked.

"You're looking through the wrong end of those astronomer's glasses," Julia said. She pointed at Alonzo's lunch, sitting in front of the window. "Look, Alonzo," she said. "You have just discovered the Pepperoni Pizza Planet!" She gave him a hug. "And I'm happy you did. Let's eat!"

Alonzo put down the pizza. He picked up the astronomer's glasses. "Glasses on," he said.

He looked out of the window behind him. Mars was a little red ball in front of the sun. "If we went to camp on Mars, we would be there by now," Alonzo said.

"We would be dead, too," said Julia. "It's so gloomy there and the atmosphere is poisonous. And don't forget the dust and windstorms. Now look out of the other window, Alonzo. I've set the computer to find the distance."

"Good," said Alonzo. He looked out of the front window. "Awesome!" he said. "What's THAT?"

"What do you see?" Julia asked.

"I think it's a sphere," Alonzo answered. "Yes, it's a giant planet."

"Is it Jupiter?" asked Julia.

"No, it isn't Jupiter," Alonzo answered. "You have to see the size of this thing. If Jupiter looked like a pea, this would be a grapefruit. It's huge. And the surface is so strange! There are big red spots everywhere. They must be volcanoes. Lots of volcanoes!"

"Alonzo," Julia said. "I don't think that a planet like that exists!"

"Just look for yourself!" said Alonzo.

PROJECT

Make your own solar system.

Work in groups. Choose one of the following ways to make a solar system.

 Here are two charts to help you to make the planets the right size and put them the right distance from one another.

If Earth were as large as an onion, Mercury would be the size of a pea.	
Mercury	pea
Venus	walnut
Mars	cherry
Jupiter	large head of lettuce
Saturn	grapefruit
Uranus	smaller head of lettuce
Neptune	orange
Pluto	apple seed

If Earth were 2.5 centimetres from the sun, Mercury would be about 0.8 centimetres from the sun.	
Mercury	0.8 cm
Venus	1.9 cm
Mars	3.75 cm
Jupiter	13.75 cm
Saturn	23.75 cm
Uranus	48.75 cm
Neptune	75 cm
Pluto	98.3 cm

1. Make a mobile of the solar system. Use a clothes hanger, paper, paints or crayons, string and scissors. Cut out circles of different sizes for the planets and the sun. Attach each planet to one end of a string. Tie the other end of string to the bottom part of the hanger.

2. Make a table model of the solar system. Use objects that show the different sizes of the planets.

3. Make a model of the solar system on paper. Cut out circles from coloured paper to show the different sizes of the planets and sun. Glue them onto paper. Label them.

✓ A trip to the planets

Saturn has seven rings.

1. Go to page 101. Work with a partner.
2. When you land on a planet, give two facts about it. If you give two correct facts, find your correct planet card and place it on the planet.
3. If you land on a planet with a card on it, you lose a turn.
4. The winner is the one with the most planet cards on the board after you both reach "Finish."

Finish

Pluto

Neptune

Start Here!

You are in a windstorm. Go forwards 3 spaces.

Venus

Mercury

You meet strange alien creatures. Go forwards 2 spaces.

Your rocket shoes push you forwards. Go forwards 2 spaces.

Earth

Sun

Mars

Uranus

A spaceship comes to save you. Go back 2 spaces.

Saturn

You smell dangerous gas fumes. Go forwards 2 spaces.

Jupiter

 Describe Jupiter's moons.

Here is a diagram of Jupiter's four largest moons.
Write sentences about their sizes and distances from Jupiter.

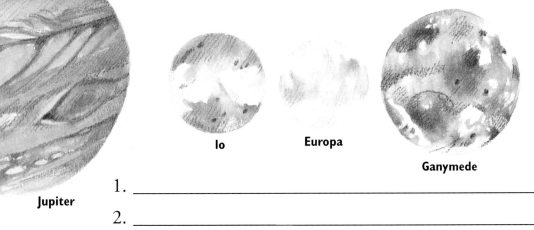

Io

Europa

Ganymede

Callisto

Jupiter

1. _____

2. _____

3. _____

4. _____

 Remember and write.

Complete these paragraphs. Use the information
you learnt in this unit.

1. If I visited Venus, _____

_____.

2. If I visited Mars, _____

_____.

My Journal

1. The most interesting fact I learnt in this unit was _____

_____.

2. After reading this unit, I would like to learn more about _____

_____.

6 Adventures

1. Think and discuss.

1. Do you like adventure stories? Why or why not?
2. If you could read one of the books shown, which would you read?
3. Have you ever had an exciting adventure? Talk about it.

2. What adventures interest you?

Complete the checklist. Mark with a ✔.

Activily	I've done this.	I'd like to do this.	I wouldn't like to do this.
1. Parachute from a plane			
2. Go mountain climbing			
3. Be in a bicycle race			
4. Learn how to sail a sailing boat			
5. Go canoeing down a river			
6.		✔	

1. Add one activity you'd like to do.
2. If you could choose only one activity, which would you do? Work with a partner and decide on one activity.

3. Read a sailing race adventure.

Look through the story. Circle any words that are new to you. Try to work out what they mean. Compare your ideas with a partner's. Then read the story and do the activities on page 54.

17 SAILING BOATS left England in September 1973 in the first round-the-world sailing race. Chay Blyth, in the British boat *Great Britain II*, faced many risks and travelled 50,000 kilometres to finish first in April 1974.

The race was on! Sailing boats from countries all over the world left Portsmouth behind and raced across the sea.

In stormy weather near the Canary Islands, waves crashed against the boats. Tabarly in the French boat *Pen Duick VI* was in first place. Blyth was second. Suddenly strong winds snapped the mast of the French boat.

If the boat stayed without a mast, Tabarly would be out of the race. *Pen Duick VI* was 1,200 miles away from Rio de Janeiro and 2,200 miles away from Cape Town. What could he do? Tabarly sent a radio message to France for a new mast. An aeroplane took the mast to Rio. Tabarly continued to race. Without a new mast, Tabarly's race might have ended near the start!

Halfway between Cape Town and Sydney, the Mexican boat *Sayula II* turned over. Water filled Carlin's boat. Luckily the boat righted itself, but Carlin was scared. If the boat stayed full of water, it would sink. For two hours, the sailors emptied the water with buckets. At last the boat was safe and Carlin could continue to race!

Between Sydney and Cape Horn a sailor on *Great Britain II* had changed a sail and was cleaning up. He fell into the sea. Blyth looked for him for three hours, but the sailor had disappeared. Sadly Blyth continued the race. *Great Britain II* was the first to go round Cape Horn and stayed in first place to the end.

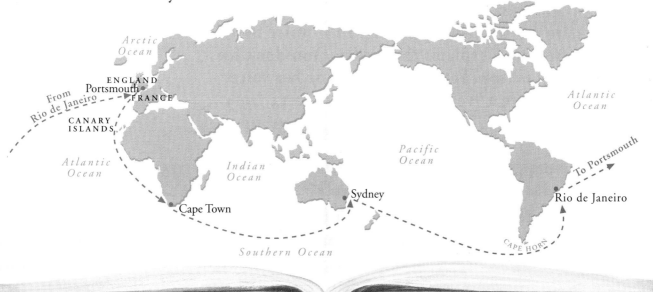

4. Complete the story board.

To make a film of the first round-the-world sailing race, a filmmaker starts with a story board. Write what is happening in each picture.

1

2

3

4

_____

_____

_____

_____

_____

_____

_____

_____

5. Make your own story board.

Choose another adventure from the sailing race. Draw scenes of the adventure. Write about what is happening in each scene. Use a separate piece of paper.

> Scene One: Dangers of a Sailing Race

6. Narrate the sailing race adventure.

Filmmakers sometimes use a "voice over" to say what is happening. In a "voice over," someone explains the actions. You don't see the person. You only hear his or her voice. Prepare a "voice over" for your scene from Activity 5. Present your work to a group.

7. Write a title for the film.

Write a title for a film about the first round-the-world sailing race. Share your title with the class. Vote for which title is the best.

_____

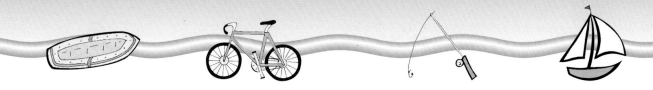

Pleasant Island

River Town Camp

Beach Bay Camping

Lost Valley Farm

Starlight Hill Campsite

1. What would you do if you visited Pleasant Island?
   Choose two activities for each camp.

   If I visited River Town Camp, I would bike and
   go to the amusement park.

Beach Bay Camping

_____

_____

Starlight Hill Campsite

_____

_____

Lost Valley Farm

_____

_____

River Town Camp

_____

_____

2. If you were able to choose only one camp on Pleasant Island,
   which camp would you choose? Why? Discuss your answer with
   your classmates. Find out the most popular place with the class.

9. What could they do?

1. Flora and José are camping on an island. A storm blows away their food and equipment. They can't be rescued until tomorrow. Work with a partner. What could they do if they had each of these things?

   2-way radio   *If they had a 2-way radio, they could call for help.*

   1. axe   2. saucepan   3. fishing rod
   4. matches   5. sleeping bags 6. torch

2. If you were in their place and could have three of the things, which three would you choose? Work with a partner and make a list.

10. Listen to the adventure story.

Fill in the chart. Work in groups to discuss the coincidence.

Name Bank: Roger   Roger's parents   Alice Blaise   Ted Blaise

Scene 1 Place: _____

People in the scene: _____

What happened: _____ saved _____.

Scene 2 Place: _____

People in the scene: _____

What happened: _____ saved _____.

11. Read the poem

Make another verse. Share it with the class.

If I Lived
If I lived on a mountain, I'd ride my bike down it.
If I lived on a lake, I'd canoe all around it.
If I lived on an island, I'd sail out to sea.
And if I weren't myself, I'd want to be me!

What's the difference between *would* and *could*?

ADVENTURE at BEAR LAKE
by Judy Nayer

Nico loved adventure. He rode on the fastest rides at the amusement park. He went down the biggest mountains on skis. He had gone snorkelling at a beach resort and horse-riding at a farm. He had hiked in the Grand Canyon and he had gone down the Mississippi River on a raft.

So, when his family said they were going to hike, camp and fish at Bear Lake, he was very excited. He had to get organised.

Nico found everything he might need. He got his boots, sleeping bag and fishing rod. He got his compass, cooking pot and torch. His mother and father got the rest of the equipment.

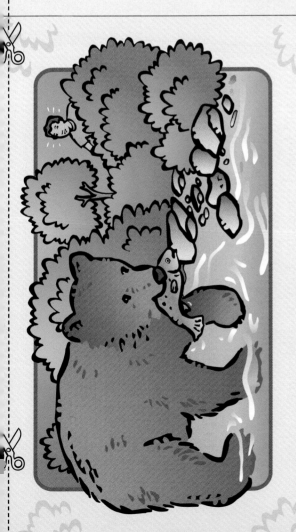

Nico turned to walk to the tent. That was when he saw the bear. Nico knew he was in danger. He had to figure out what to do. "If I ran, would it chase me?" he asked himself. He decided it was too big a risk. Then Nico had an idea. He took the fish he had caught and threw it in the lake. The bear saw it. Nico watched the bear pass by. Suddenly the bear took the fish out of the water. As the bear ate, Nico ran to the tent. His mother and father were still sleeping. Nico woke them up and told them all about the bear. From a safe distance, they watched the bear go into the mountains.

Nico stayed at the campsite that day. He still loved adventure. But meeting a wild bear was a little more adventure than he wanted.

They got the map and started the drive up the mountains. It was a long trip. When they got to the campsite, it was dark. But Nico could tell the location was wonderful. They were on Bear Lake. "There are lots of fish in that lake," he thought. Nico's father put up the tent. Then he got the matches and started a fire. Nico loved being outdoors. He was too excited to sleep.

Nico did sleep, but he got up before the sun. He could not wait. He took his fishing rod and went down to the lake.

The red canoe looked as if it were waiting in the water just for him. Nico got in and started to canoe across the lake. He was careful not to go far. If he could see the campsite, he would not get lost. He took out his fishing rod. In a few minutes, he caught a fish! Nico watched the fish leap in the air. He almost made the canoe tip over as he got the fish in the canoe.

Nico began to think. "If Mother and Father got up and found me gone, they would worry." Nico decided to hurry back to the campsite. He got the canoe out of the lake.

PROJECT

INA AND HER BROTHER, Billy, were visiting Lost Valley Farm. One afternoon they wanted to go horse-riding. Ina and Billy were good riders, so their parents said it was OK. Ina and Billy promised to stay near the camp and return by seven o'clock. They took a map and some food for a snack and went off.

Ina and Billy were riding slowly through the hills when they saw a wild horse. They decided to chase it. The race was on—for a short time. The horse was too fast and was soon far away. Ina and Billy stopped and tied their horses to a tree. They looked at the map, but they couldn't work out where they were. They were lost!

They decided to walk to the top of a hill. Perhaps they could see something familiar. But they didn't see anything they knew. When they got back, the horses were gone! They hadn't tied them up well enough.

There they were. All they had were a map and their snacks. And it was getting dark. What could they do?

How would you rescue them?

1. Work with a partner. What could Ina and Billy do if they had any one of these things?

   compass   **2-way radio**
   matches   **mirror**

2. With your partner, make up an ending for the story.

Complete-the-sentence race

1. Follow the instructions on page 103 to get ready for the game.
2. Work in groups of three.
3. Taking turns, Student 1 picks a game card from the cup, reads the incomplete sentence and makes up endings. Student 1 has *one minute* to make up as many complete sentences as possible. Each sentence earns one point.
4. Student 2 times Student 1. Student 3 keeps score on the score card.
5. The person with the most points at the end of each round wins.

> If I had skis, I could ski down a mountain.

Used Cards

Complete the sentences.

Use *if* and *would* or *could*.

live in the mountains
If I lived in the mountains, I would ski every day.

1. be able to fly anywhere in the world

   _____

2. live near the North Pole

   _____

3. have a racing bike

   _____

4. be able to have an exciting adventure

   _____

What would you do?

**There are many things to do at a winter resort.
Write what you would like to do if you
were at one.**

_____

_____

_____

_____

My Journal

1. The best adventure film I've ever seen is _____.

2. An adventure story I would like to read is _____.

3. The most exciting adventure I read about in this unit was _____

   _____.

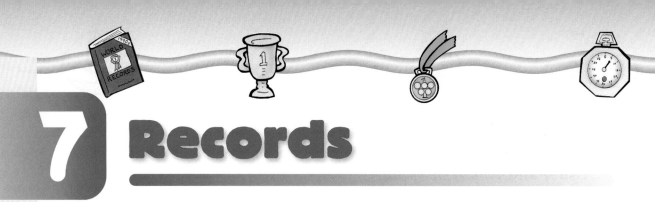

7 Records

1. Think and discuss.

A competition is a game or race to see who can win.
1. Have you ever been in a competition?
2. Have you ever won a prize of any kind?

Fun Fact
Diane Witt of the United States has the world's longest hair. It's 3.7 metres long.

2. Listen. Read.

The country with the fewest people in the world is the Vatican City. It has 1,000 people.

Act out the conversation.

Julia and Tom are practising for a geography competition at school. The category of questions is "Cities and Towns."

Julia: Let's begin. Jericho.
Tom: What's the oldest city in the world?
Julia: Correct. Tokyo.
Tom: Oh, I know that. What's the city in the world that has the most people?
Julia: Good. London.
Tom: That's easy. What is the largest city in Europe?
Julia: Try this one. Wenzhuan, China.
Tom: Wenzhuan? Oh, I know. What's the lowest town in the world?
Julia: Sorry. Wenzhuan is the highest town in the world.

3. Discuss with a partner. Read.

Skim the book review to find the answers.

1. What do you know about *The Guinness Book of World Records*?
2. What categories does it contain?
3. Who was the tallest person?

Language Note

most + noun
most languages

fewest + noun
fewest people

RECORDS, RECORDS AND MORE RECORDS

The Guinness Book of World Records was first printed in England on August 27, 1955. Now it's published in twenty-seven languages and is one of the most popular books in the world.

This book contains records of every kind. They are arranged in categories, such as Science and Technology, Living World, Arts and Entertainment, Human Achievements and Sports and Games.

Do you think you could get into *The Guinness Book of World Records*? Every year, the editors list several categories they are interested in writing about. Here are some examples:

Oldest human being:

Do you know anyone who is more than 105 years old? A recent record holder was 122 years old.

Tallest human being:

Do you know anyone more than 2.5 metres tall? The tallest human on record was Robert Wadlow. He was 2.72 metres tall.

The most accomplished linguist:

Can you speak the most languages fluently? The current record holder speaks 22 languages.

The most bottles collected and recycled by a group:

There is no current record. It's up to you!

If you haven't already seen *The Guinness Book of World Records*, I suggest you go to your nearest bookshop or library and get a copy. A new edition comes out every year. Some people might say it is the greatest book around.

4. Read and match.

Compare your answers in small groups.

Read the categories in *The Guinness Book of World Records.* Then read the questions and decide where you would find each answer. Write the number of the category on the line.

The answers are all in this unit!

Categories
1. Living World (Plants and Animals)
2. Human Beings
3. Science and Technology
4. Arts and Entertainment
5. Human World and Achievements
6. Sports and Games

Fun Fact

The first person to swim the English Channel was Matthew Webb, on August 24 and 25, 1875.

_____ 1. How long is Diane Witt's hair?

_____ 2. What's the longest time someone spent walking on a tightrope?

_____ 3. How fast can the quickest insect run?

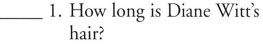

_____ 4. Which city has the most telephones?

_____ 5. Where was the largest painting in the world?

_____ 6. What's the most miles a car has travelled?

_____ 7. Which country in the world has the fewest people?

_____ 8. When did the first person swim the English Channel?

5. Listen. Fill in the chart.

Gary Sobers is a famous cricketer. Listen to the report and write the numbers in the chart.

Gary Sobers

year of birth   _____

year first played for his country   _____

number of runs for his country   _____

number of catches for his country _____

6. Find out about sports stars.

Work with a partner. Student A uses the information on this page, and Student B uses the information on page 66.

Student A: Think of questions and ask your partner about Nadia Comaneci. Fill in the chart. Answer your partner's questions.

Nadia Comaneci

year of birth   _____

number of perfect scores   _____

number of Olympic medals   _____

age when she won
Olympic medals   _____

A World Cup Hero

Edison Arantes do Nascimento—Pelé—is the greatest football player of all time. He was born in Brazil in 1940. In 1958, when he was only seventeen, he was a hero of the World Cup championship. Pelé played in two more World Cup championship teams for Brazil in 1962 and 1970. In 1970, he became the highest-paid football player in the world. He retired in 1977 after playing 1,363 games and scoring 1,281 goals.

Student B: Think of questions and ask your partner about Pelé. Fill in the chart. Answer your partner's questions.

Pelé

year of birth   _____

age at first championship   _____

number of World Cup championships   _____

number of goals   _____

Fun Fact

The world's largest painting was done by students in New South Wales, Australia. It measured 6736.6 square metres.

A True Champion

An Olympic first happened in gymnastics in 1976. Nadia Comaneci, born in Romania in 1961, performed on the asymmetric bars and the judges gave her a perfect score of 10. After that performance, Nadia went on to earn another six perfect 10 scores—three more on the asymmetric bars and three on the beam. By the end of the Olympics, Nadia had won a total of five medals—three gold, a silver and a bronze. Nadia was only fourteen years old!

save = to stop a goal

7. Listen and sing.

Take me out to the football match,
Take me out to the crowd.
Buy me a drink and some crisps to eat,
Then into the ground to find our seat.
So it's cheer, cheer, cheer for the home team,
If they don't win it's a shame.
But it's goals, saves, excitement we've come to see,
A good football game.

Fun Fact

The fastest insect in the world is the cockroach. It can travel at 3.4 miles (5.4 kilometres) per hour, or 50 body lengths per second.

ATALANTA'S RACE

A Greek Myth Re-told by Fullerton M. Bright

Once there was a girl named Atalanta. She was very beautiful! She had a face like a perfect silver flower. Most men loved her. But Atalanta saw no one she wanted for a husband. To keep all the men at a distance, she announced a competition.

"I will run a race," she said. "My goal is to win. But some hero may be faster than I am. If he wins, he will earn, not a championship or a medal, but a wife. Me!" Then she told them what would happen if they lost. "If I win, you will pay the highest price," she said. "You will be dead before morning."

Hippomenes threw the largest apple last. It was heavy, but Atalanta picked it up. Atalanta ran her slowest race ever. Hippomenes finished in front of her.

"I have won the race and the prize," Hippomenes told Atalanta. "Now you are mine."

Atalanta smiled. "And you are mine," she said.

So Hippomenes and Atalanta became husband and wife.

Did they live perfect lives? Were they happy ever after?

No, no. But that is a different story.

Most men loved their lives too much to run that race. But a few still wanted to try. So Atalanta arranged a race.

Now, Hippomenes could not participate in the race. He was to judge the contest. But when he saw Atalanta, he wanted the prize for himself. "Win, Atalanta!" he thought as he watched her run. "Win, Win!"

And she did. She was a perfect runner—the best! She finished far ahead of the others.

"Now I want to race with you," Hippomenes told her. Atalanta looked at him. Like her, Hippomenes was very handsome.

"I suggest you don't run. I do not want to kill you," Atalanta said. "But I will if I have to." Hippomenes knew it would be the hardest race ever. He asked Venus, who had special powers, to help him. Venus gave Hippomenes three gold apples. They were perfect apples. He knew just what to do with them.

The race began. Atalanta was soon in front. Hippomenes threw an apple to one side. Atalanta saw the perfect gold fruit. She stopped to pick it up. Hippomenes ran past her. Twice more Atalanta was in front. Twice more Hippomenes threw a gold apple.

PROJECT

Plan a classroom "Olympics."

1. Think of activities for the class to do. Share your ideas with your classmates. Vote for the best ideas. Look at the examples at the right.

2. Organise your Olympics. What day will the games take place? Who can participate? Where can the students sign up? What materials will you need for the activities? Who will judge the competitions? Who will keep score? What will the prizes be?

- Who can throw a piece of paper in the wastepaper basket the most times without missing?

- Who can spell the most words in English without making a mistake?

- Who can guess how many beans are in a jar?

- Who can jump the furthest?

- Who can juggle tennis balls the most times?

- Who can say the tongue twister "Seven super sports stars" the most times?

The city with the most telephones is Tokyo, Japan.

Fun Fact

The most miles ever driven in a car was 1,442,044 miles (2,326,482 kilometres). The car was a Volkswagen "Beetle."

Make a Record Book.

Include the names of the winners of your Olympics.

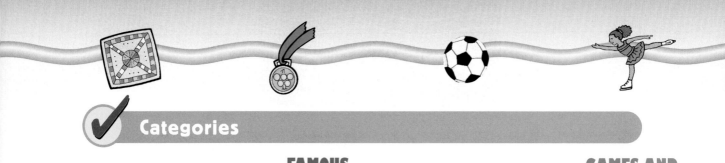

✓ Categories

	SCIENCE	FAMOUS PEOPLE	MISCELLANEOUS	GAMES AND SPORTS
1				
2				
3				
4				

1. Play in a group of three—two players and a host. The host puts the answers from page 105 face-down on the board.
2. Players take turns choosing a category and a number. They read the answer and make up a question.
3. If a player doesn't make up a correct question, the other player can try. Each correct question wins one point. The player with the most points wins.

> The longest time spent walking on a tightrope is 185 days.

Write about your personal records.

IDEA BOX

time spent talking on the phone   distance travelled on a bike in one day

number of biscuits eaten in one day   time spent playing video games in one day

The highest score I've ever got in an English test is 100.
The lowest score I've ever got in an English test is 60.

1. _____

2. _____

3. _____

4. _____

Write information questions.

You are reporting on your classroom Olympics. Write three questions you would ask to get information for your article.

1. _____

2. _____

3. _____

My Journal

1. My favourite sports star is _____

    because _____.

2. The best part of this unit is _____

    because _____.

3. Now I can talk about _____.

8 Symbols

1. Think and discuss.

1. Can you express an idea without using words? Give an example.
2. What signs do you see every day that do not use words? Give an example.

2. Learn about body language.

Here are some examples of body language. They are used by people in English-speaking countries.

1. What time is it?

2. I don't know.

3. Wish me luck!

What might each mean? Look at page 107 for the answers.

1.

2.

3.

Can you use gestures to express the meanings in the pictures? Which gestures are the same in your culture? Which are different?

Language Note

It might mean . . .

It could mean . . .

It must mean . . .

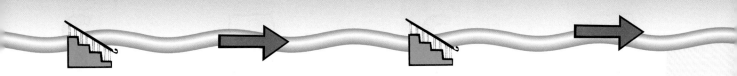

3. Listen. Read.

Act out the conversation.

Using symbols is another way of expressing yourself without words. Amy used symbols in the message on the right, which she wrote for Tracey and Alec. What might the message mean?

TRACEY: Why don't we start from the top? That must be the start. The first picture looks like steps.

ALEC: With an arrow pointing down. It must mean that she's gone *downstairs*. What about the next picture?

TRACEY: Hmmm. Is that an eye?

ALEC: It might mean that she went downstairs to look at something.

TRACEY: The next pictures are faces, aren't they?

ALEC: I know! She went downstairs to look at faces.

TRACEY: That doesn't make sense. I think the faces are masks.

ALEC: Amy went to see the masks in the art show!

TRACEY: We could go down to the art room and see if she's there.

ALEC: Let's go!

> **Making Suggestions**
> Why don't we go? =
> We could go =
> Let's go

4. Work with messages in symbols.

1. What does the message below mean? Complete the instructions.

1. Go out of the classroom to the water fountain.   2. Then . . .

2. Work with a partner. Write a message in code. Exchange messages with another pair. Can they understand your message?

5. Do you know about codes?

You have seen how you can use symbols to "write" without words. You also can write in code.

Here is a message written in code. How does the code work?

Here's a hint!
1. Write a sentence.
2. Then write each word again. This time write each word backwards.

ll'I teem uoy ta ruo terces gnidih ecalp.

I'll meet you at our secret hiding place.

Many messages are written in alphabet code. You need to use the alphabet to work out the code. Can you break this alphabet code? What's the secret message?

Use these instructions to work out the message.
1. Write the alphabet. Under each alphabet letter, write the letter that comes after it. For example, under A write B, under B write C, and so on. For Z, write A.
2. Use this alphabet code to "translate" each letter in the message. For example, U stands for T and P stands for O. So UP is the word "TO."

DPNF UP B
QBSUZ BU NZ
IPVTF.

Think of a secret message to send to a partner in one of the codes on this page. Exchange messages and decode them.

6. Invent your own code.

Work with a partner.

1. Make up your own code.
2. Write instructions for your code.
3. Write a secret message in the code.
4. Exchange messages and code instructions with other partners. Each pair should decode the message received.

7. Can you understand the code!

Follow these instructions to fill in the chart. Then use the code to read the secret message.

It's as easy as ABC.

Hint: A is 11,
B is 12,
K is 33.

Secret Message:
1343142153 115221 226142!

Meaning:_____

Middle Column ↓

	1	2		←Row
1	A		C	
3		J		
5				
		Z		

8. Can you read picture writing?

Ancient Egyptian
Water

Native American
Spring

Aztec (Mexican)
Rain

International Sign
Telephone to the right

Many years ago before people invented alphabets, they used picture messages. Pictures stood for words. People still use picture messages. What might each picture below mean? Look at page 107 for the answers.

Ancient Egyptian

Native American

Aztec (Mexican)

International Sign

9. Be a sign detective.

Look for signs without words in the places you know. Draw them on a piece of paper. Share them with the class.

10. Do colours have meanings?

In English-speaking countries, colour words have various meanings. Red, of course, means "Stop." You see it on traffic lights. Red also has a lot of power or impact. Red objects stand out.

In contrast to red, green means "Go." It also stands for spring and newness and things that are growing.

Blue is a "cool" colour, like green. It often stands for sadness. You have heard of blues music, haven't you?

Work with a partner. What do colours mean in your culture? Complete the chart.

Colour	Meanings
_____	_____
_____	_____
_____	_____

11. Learn about idioms with colours.

English has many idioms. Idioms are phrases that have got a special meaning. This meaning can be different from the meaning of the words themselves. Can you guess the meaning of the idioms in **dark print**? Match the colour idioms with their definitions.

1. Martin has **green fingers**. His plants are always beautiful.

A. *the OK to go*

2. Josefina feels **blue**. She did not do well in the competition.

B. *ability to grow things well*

3. When I forget to clean my room, my parents **see red**. They don't like it and they let me know it.

C. *sad or depressed*

4. When the coach gave me the **green light**, I started to run.

D. *get angry*

Lost in the Jungle

By Theresa Meghan

Cam said to Jess, "It's going to rain. Let's stay inside. Why don't we finish reading our book? It's my turn to read."

Cam and Jess were reading a story about a boy named Ben who got lost on a trip to the rain forest with his family.

Cam's fingers moved over the row of Braille symbols as she read.

"Ben was hungry, thirsty and scared. He was alone in the middle of the jungle, where some of the wildest animals in the world lived. A tiger could spring out at him! He might see a snake!"

Cam read. "'The arrow flew past Ben's ear. Ben fainted. When he opened his eyes, he was looking into his father's face.

"'Ben!' Dad said. 'I am so happy we found you! This man was helping us to look for you. He and a giant snake found you at the same time. He killed the snake with an arrow just as it was about to attack you!'"

"Cam," Jess said. "I'm so happy you know Braille. This book is even more scary in the dark!"

Cam and Jess laughed. Lightning lit the room and Cam turned to the next story.

Jess and Cam heard thunder. A storm was coming.

Cam read louder. "'Ben picked a ripe mango and ate it. It was delicious. But Ben still felt thirsty. "I'm not going to find a water fountain here," he said to himself. "Or a sign giving directions to a town. I have no idea where I am."'"

Then it was Jess's turn to read.

"'Just then, Ben heard a sound behind him,'" he read. "'He turned to look. There was a man with an ancient face.'" Thunder roared. Jess had to shout to be heard.

"'The man made a wild gesture. But Ben couldn't understand the man's body language. What was he trying to say? Then the man began to shout. Afraid, Ben walked backwards a few steps.

'Suddenly the man pulled out an arrow.'"

Just then there was a flash of lightning. The lights in the house went out.

"No!" Jess said. "Cam, the lights went out! And this is the most exciting scene! What do you think might happen? Will you read now?"

"Don't worry, Jess," Cam said. "My fingers don't need lights to read."

PROJECT

What Is Orange?
by Mary O'Neill

Orange is a tiger lily,
A carrot,
A feather from
A parrot,
A flame,
The wildest colour
You can name.

Orange is an orange
Also a mango.
Orange is music
of the tango.

Orange is the fur
Of the fiery fox,
The brightest crayon
In the box.

And in the fall
When leaves are turning,
Orange is the smell
Of a bonfire burning . . . .

fall = autumn

Read the poem again. Copy the chart. Show
how the poet helps you to see, hear, smell, taste
and feel the colour orange.

See	Hear	Smell	Taste	Feel
A hot flame	_____	_____	_____	_____

Can you write a colour poem?

Red is a stop sign.
It's a poppy,
A ripe tomato,
A warm winter jacket,
A dancing flame.
It's the boldest colour
You can name.

Work with a group.
Choose another colour.
Fill in the chart at the
right.

Write your own poem
about a colour.

Colour_____

Things with the Colour

_____

_____

_____

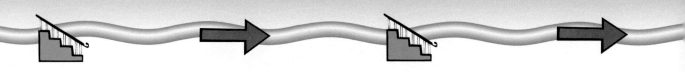

✓ What's the message?

1. Go to page 107. Cut out the symbols.
2. Use the symbols to make a message. Place the message in the boxes below. You can draw additional symbols in the blank boxes.
3. Then work with a partner. Give your partner instructions to place the same symbols as yours in the same boxes. Give your partner instructions on how to draw any new symbols you added.
4. Can your partner guess the meaning of your message?
5. Now it's your partner's turn to give instructions.

What could it mean?

Can you get the message?

Write down what you think the instructions mean.

_____

_____

Can you work out the code?

Read the message.

Hint: This is an alphabet code. Each letter stands for another letter. The letter used most often in this message is E.

XNT QDZKKX TMCDQRSZMC SGDRD BNCDR

_____

Write the instructions for the code.

_____

_____

_____

_____

My Journal

1. Now that I have completed this unit, I know that I can communicate without words by using _____

_____ .

2. The most interesting thing I learnt in this unit was _____

_____ .

9 On Stage

Variety is the spice of life.

1. Think and discuss.

1. What is a variety show? What kinds of entertainers might you see on a TV variety show?
2. Have you ever performed in front of a group? What did you do? What talents have you got?

2. Listen. Read.

Act out the conversation.

Jenny: Did you see "Variety Time" on TV last night?

Tara: I did. Wasn't it wonderful?

Jenny: Wonderful? I thought it was awful!

Hal: How can you say that? The magician was brilliant! I really liked it when he made the elephant disappear.

Tara: Yes. And Looby Loo was superb! She sang all my favourite songs.

Jenny: But she sang them badly! She has a horrible voice!

Hal: Well, what about that comedian, Joey Black? I thought his jokes were really funny.

Jenny: They were dreadful. They weren't very funny and I'd heard them all before.

Tara: Jenny, if you hated the show so much, why did you watch it?

Jenny: Oh, I was babysitting for my little sisters and they wanted to see it. I wanted to watch the film on Channel 4.

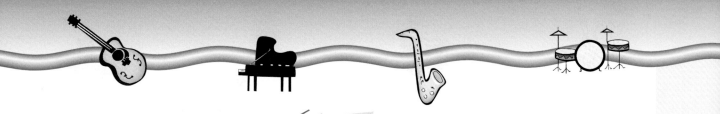

3. State your opinion.

Synonyms are words that mean almost the same.
Work with a partner. Read the synonyms for *good* and *bad*.
Use the synonyms to answer the questions below.

They are good dancers.

They are bad dancers.
They need more practice.

Synonyms

good	**very good**	bad	**very bad**
wonderful		awful	
fantastic		terrible	
brilliant		horrible	
superb		ghastly	
magnificent	**very, very good**	dreadful	**very, very bad**

1. Who's your favourite singer? What do you think of that singer's talent?
2. What's your least favourite TV programme? What do you think of it?
3. What's the last film you saw? What did you think of it?

4. What's a good review?

Read the review of "Variety Time." Then pretend you are
Jenny from Activity 2. Write her review of the show.

Last night "Variety Time" was the best show on television! Looby Loo was, as usual, superb. She sang brilliantly. Presto the Magician was very entertaining. He made an elephant disappear right in front of everyone's eyes! And the new young comedian Joey Black was hilarious. He's going to have a fantastic career!

5. Do a talent survey.

Your class is going to have a talent show. Look at the list of talents. What are you good at? If your talent isn't listed, write it in the chart.

Talent	Class Survey
Sing	
Dance	
Tell jokes	
Act	
Do magic tricks	
Recite a poem	
Mime	
Say tongue twisters	
Play a musical instrument	

> I'll make magnificent music!

1. Choose one or two things you are good at and write them on a piece of paper.
2. Do a class survey. Ask two students to collect the papers and read the talents aloud. Under **Class Survey** make a mark (/) for each talent mentioned. Count to find out how many performers your class has for each talent.

6. Make a performance badge.

1. Make a badge like the one on this page. Write one or two talents you would like to do for the talent show. Decorate your badge.
2. Go around the class. Find out other students' talents.
3. Form groups of six. Make sure each group has different talents.

Matilda
I'll do magic tricks.

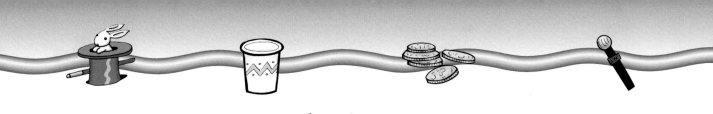

7. Learn a magic trick.

Follow the instructions. Practise until you can do the trick easily. Can you do other tricks?

The Moving Coin Trick

Before You Go on Stage

You need two paper or plastic cups, a coin and a table or desk.

1. Cut a hole in the bottom of one of the cups.
The hole should be big enough for the coin to go through.

2. Put the cup with the hole inside the other cup.

In Front of the Audience

1. Put the coin into the stack of cups.

2. Tell the audience, "I'm going to make the coin move."

3. Pull up the top cup. Make sure the coin is in the bottom cup.

4. Put the top cup on the table or desk next to the bottom cup.

5. Ask the audience, "Which cup is the coin in?"
They will point to the first cup!

6. Show the audience that the coin is in the second cup.
The audience will be surprised!

8. Listen to comedy acts!

**Who are the characters in the jokes? Circle all the answers.
Then ask the class to vote for the best joke.**

1. **Sara's joke:**   a frog   a waiter   an elephant

2. **Peter's joke:**   a boy   an elephant   a father

3. **Andrea's joke:**   a scientist   a daughter   a mother

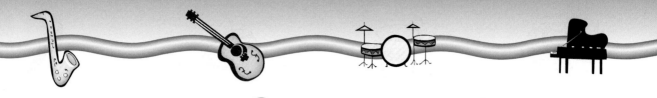

9. Listen and sing.

You might sing one of these songs in the talent show.
Or choose any other English song you know.

The Talent Show

Hey, did you hear?
The news is really great!
Our school is going to have
a talent show!
Make sure you sign up,
You don't want to be late.
It's a chance to help your
talent grow.

There's A Mountain Behind My House

There's a mountain behind my house.
I see it each day if the weather is fair.
There's a mountain behind my house,
And I'm going to climb it because it is there.

I'll fill up my backpack.
I'll put on my cap,
Take a bottle of water,
A compass, a map,
An apple, an orange,
A blanket that's grey,
And I'll climb to the top,
By the end of the day.

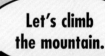

Let's climb
the mountain.

THE VARIETY SHOW

by Judy Veramendi

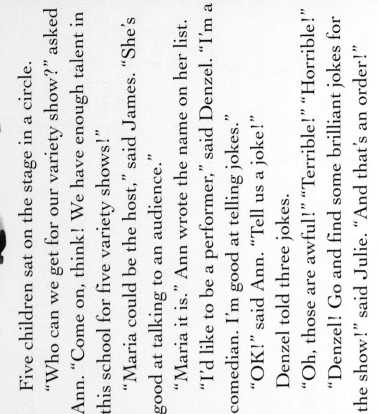

Five children sat on the stage in a circle.

"Who can we get for our variety show?" asked Ann. "Come on, think! We have enough talent in this school for five variety shows!"

"Maria could be the host," said James. "She's good at talking to an audience."

"Maria it is." Ann wrote the name on her list.

"I'd like to be a performer," said Denzel. "I'm a comedian. I'm good at telling jokes."

"OK!" said Ann. "Tell us a joke!"

Denzel told three jokes.

"Oh, those are awful!" "Terrible!" "Horrible!"

"Denzel! Go and find some brilliant jokes for the show!" said Julie. "And that's an order!"

VARIETY SHOW REVIEW

May 9

The school's variety show was a fantastic show of talent.

The magic tricks by Marco the Magnificent were wonderful.

Denzel the comedian was hilarious, and the folk singer Julie was superb. The mime was brilliant!

The host was wonderful at entertaining the audience between acts.

We have just one question: Can we have a new variety show every month?

"When do you want to rehearse?" asked Ann.

"What do you think about Tuesday, Wednesday and Thursday?" asked James.

"I have to babysit my sister on Tuesdays," said Peter. "But I can arrange for my brother to do it."

"Good. Now think—we need to find performers," said Ann.

"How about Marco the Magnificent?" asked Julie.

"Who is *that*?" asked James.

"You know, Mark Green, the magician. He does wonderful tricks," said Ann. "He can make coins disappear."

"And Tomás loves to do mime," said Julie.

"What about you, Julie?" asked Peter. "You're good at playing the guitar and singing folk songs."

"You are, Julie? I didn't know that," said Ann.

"Well, I'm not that good," said Julie.

"Yes, you are!" said Peter. "Come on, I think we've got enough entertainers. Now let's go and invite them to perform."

2
3

PROJECT

What's in the show?

Here's a programme for a class talent show.
Work with your group from Activity 6.

1. What do you think of the order of the performances?
   How would you arrange them better?
2. List some refreshments you could serve at
   your talent show.

It's Show-Off Time

Programme

"Hello, Hello! Welcome to the Class Show!"

"Get in the Mood for Fun"
     (folk song with guitar)

"The Magic Light" (dance)

"The Big Sound" (piano solo)

Interval: Refreshments served

The Joker (joke telling)

The Disappearing Coin (magic trick)

Blowing in the Wind (mime)

"There's a Mountain Behind My House" (song)

Entire class

Ricardo Ramos

Geraldine Lopez

Yana Lei

Manny Lake

Yoshi Tishi

Jane Ferrante

Entire class

Write a review.

Imagine that you have just seen the talent show. Write a review of
the show. Say if you liked the show and describe which performers
were good and which were bad.

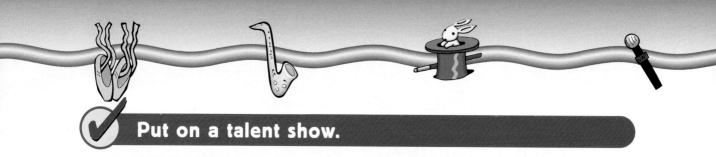

✓ Put on a talent show.

Work with your group from Activity 6.

1. Decide what each performer in the talent show will do. Write a list.

_____

_____

_____

_____

_____

_____

2. Decide the order of the performances. Use the blank programme on page 109 to make a programme for your show.
3. Decide if you will serve refreshments. What will they be? Who will bring them?
4. Decide who will be the host of your show. The host can also be a performer.
5. Practise your acts.
6. Perform the show for the class.

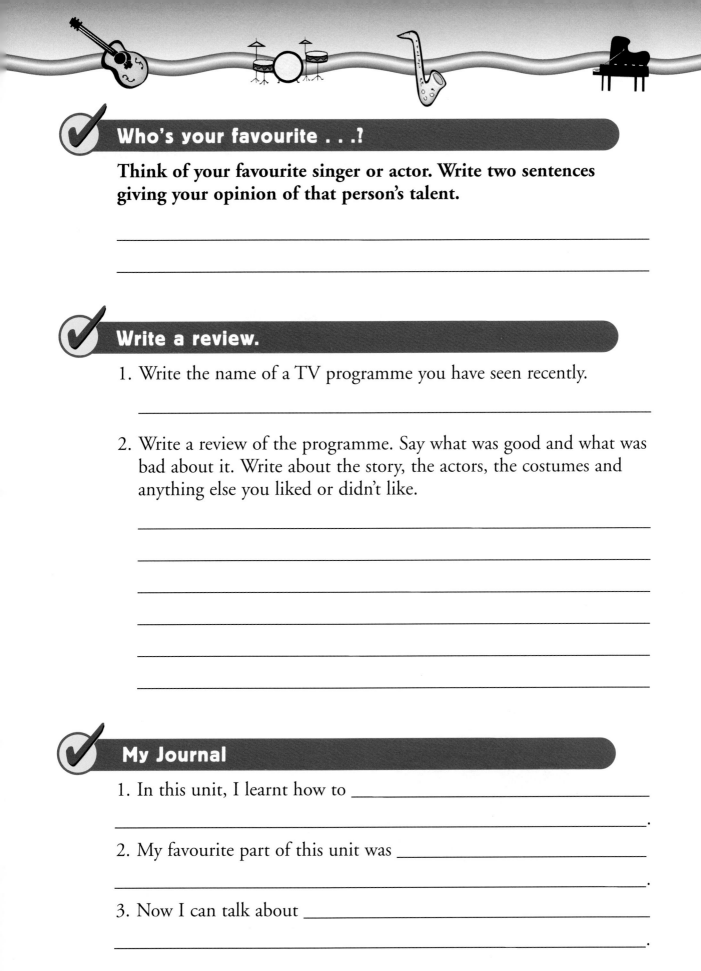

Who's your favourite . . .?

Think of your favourite singer or actor. Write two sentences giving your opinion of that person's talent.

_____

_____

Write a review.

1. Write the name of a TV programme you have seen recently.

_____

2. Write a review of the programme. Say what was good and what was bad about it. Write about the story, the actors, the costumes and anything else you liked or didn't like.

_____

_____

_____

_____

_____

_____

My Journal

1. In this unit, I learnt how to _____

_____.

2. My favourite part of this unit was _____

_____.

3. Now I can talk about _____

_____.

My Time Line

Year I was born

_____

2

Counters

Game Cards

go to a concert
Go forwards
3 spaces.

eat snails
Go forwards
4 spaces.

see a snake
Go forwards
2 spaces.

go to another
country
Go forwards 4 spaces.

go to the beach
Go forwards
1 space.

visit a museum
Go forwards
3 spaces.

go on a class trip
Go forwards
1 space.

go on a train
Go forwards
3 spaces.

see a famous person
Go forwards
4 spaces.

buy a present
for a teacher
Go forwards 2 spaces.

act in a play
Go forwards
2 spaces.

play the guitar
Go forwards
3 spaces.

go to a football match
Go forwards
3 spaces.

play basketball
Go forwards
2 spaces.

play the piano
Go forwards
2 spaces.

win first place
in a competition
Go forward 3 spaces.

see a shooting star
Go forwards
3 spaces.

lose something
important
Go back 2 spaces.

make a meal
Go forwards
3 spaces.

forget to do your
homework
Go back 2 spaces.

3

Skill Cards

Cut out the cards. Choose seven skill cards for the game.

work on a computer	create new ideas	work with tools	draw
work carefully	speak in front of people	sell things and ideas	play sports
help other people	write	teach other people how to do things	work with numbers

Counters

Stars

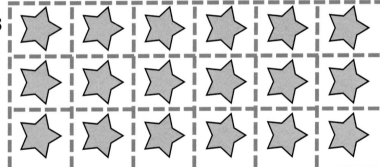

Number Cards

Cut out the cards. Put them into a cup. Pick these cards to see how many spaces to move forwards.

1	1	1	2	2
2	2	3	3	3

Time Capsule

Do Not Open Until the Year _____

This time capsule was made in the year _____.
It was made by the students of _____ School.
It shows life in the year _____.

Names of students:

_____ _____
_____ _____
_____ _____
_____ _____
_____ _____
_____ _____
_____ _____
_____ _____
_____ _____

Our message to the students of the future:

_____
_____
_____
_____
_____
_____
_____
_____
_____
_____

Number Cards

Cut out the cards. Put them into a cup. Pick these cards to see how many spaces to move forwards.

1	**1**	**1**	**2**	**2**
2	**2**	**3**	**3**	**3**

Planet Cards

Cut out the planet cards. You choose one colour to play with and your partner chooses the other colour. Use the cards in the game.

Mercury	Venus	Earth
Mars	Jupiter	Saturn
Uranus	Neptune	Pluto

Counters

Mercury	Venus	Earth
Mars	Jupiter	Saturn
Uranus	Neptune	Pluto

Game Cards

Cut out the game cards. Put them into a cup.

If I went in a submarine, ___.	If I got lost in the woods, ___.	If I travelled round the world, ___.
If I had skis, ___.	If I had a sleeping bag, ___.	If I were a bicycle racer, ___.
If I had a canoe, ___.	If I had a sailing boat, ___.	If I fell out of a boat, ___.
If I were in a snowstorm, ___.	If I saw a snake, ___.	If I were an astronaut, ___.
If I had a million pounds, ___.	If I had my own plane, ___.	If I were twenty-one years old, ___.
If I lived in space, ___.	If I went deep-sea diving, ___.	If I were at the beach, ___.

Score Card

Points

Name	Round 1	Round 2	Round 3

7

Instructions for Game Cards

1. Make up some questions and write the answers on the blank cards. Use this book, an encyclopaedia, *The Guinness Book of World Records*, or any other reliable source to make sure the answers are correct.

2. Cut out the cards and place them face-down on the game board. Put the answers under the correct categories. Here are some examples.

Answer: Pluto
Question: What is the coldest planet? (Science Category)

Answer: A dog made of plasticine.
Question: Who is Gromit? (Miscellaneous Category)

Game Cards

ANSWER	ANSWER	ANSWER	ANSWER
ANSWER	ANSWER	ANSWER	ANSWER
ANSWER	ANSWER	ANSWER	ANSWER
ANSWER	ANSWER	ANSWER	ANSWER

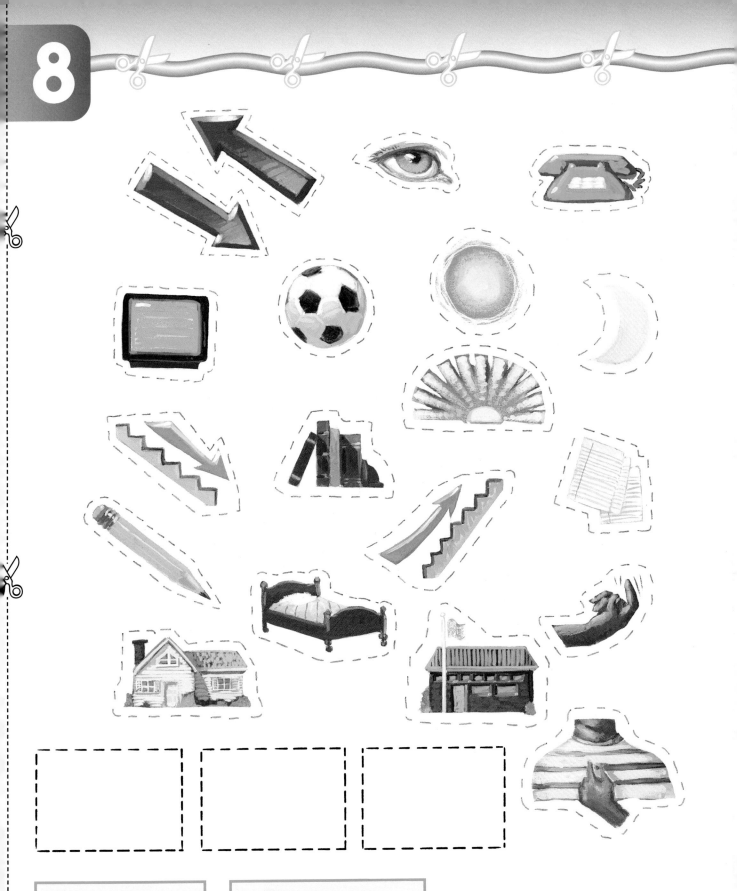

8

Answers for Page 72

1. I know the answer!
2. This smells terrible.
3. I can't hear you.

Answers for Page 75

Egyptian: Rain
Native American: Summer
Aztec: Snake
Sign: Restaurant

Title of Show

Programme

Title of Piece   **Performer**

Interval: Refreshments served